The Nutrient Cycle

Lisa Greathouse

Consultant

Jill Tobin
California Teacher of the Year
Semi-Finalist
Burbank Unified School District

Publishing Credits

Rachelle Cracchiolo, M.S.Ed., *Publisher*
Conni Medina, M.A.Ed., *Managing Editor*
Diana Kenney, M.A.Ed., NBCT, *Senior Editor*
Dona Herweck Rice, *Series Developer*
Robin Erickson, *Multimedia Designer*
Timothy Bradley, *Illustrator*

Image Credits: Cover, p.1 All Canada Photos/Alamy; p.19 Courtney Patterson; pp.4, 5, 8, 12, 14, 15, 16, 18, 19, 20, 21, 23, 24, 30, 32 iStock; pp.10, 11 Monique Domínguez; pp.13, 25, 28, 29 Timothy J. Bradley; all other images from Shutterstock.

Library of Congress Cataloging-in-Publication Data

Greathouse, Lisa E., author.
  The Nutrient cycle / Lisa Greathouse.
    pages cm
  Summary: "Living things depend on a few invisible but essential nutrients to survive. These nutrients each have their own purpose. But they are also interconnected in the nutrient cycle"-- Provided by publisher.
  Audience: Grades 4-6.
  Includes index.
  ISBN 978-1-4807-4680-0 (pbk.) -- ISBN 1-4807-4680-0 (pbk.)
  1. Biogeochemical cycles--Juvenile literature. 2. Carbon cycle (Biogeochemistry)--Juvenile literature. 3. Nitrogen cycle--Juvenile literature. 4. Hydrologic cycle--Juvenile literature. I. Title.
  QH344.G74 2016
  577.14--dc23
                          2014045203

Teacher Created Materials

5301 Oceanus Drive
Huntington Beach, CA 92649-1030
http://www.tcmpub.com

ISBN 978-1-4807-4680-0

Table of Contents

Nutrient Cycle

It's important to recycle to protect the environment. But did you know nature recycles every day? Nature takes old and used substances and turns them into things that can be used again. Recycling may come in the form of water that pours from a rain cloud into a lake. It may be found in a leaf that drops from a tree to the ground and becomes food for the soil. It may be found on a larger scale when a squirrel dies and it becomes dinner for a fox. This is the cycle of life. And it must stay in balance.

All living things require a few key **nutrients**. The nutrient cycle describes how these key ingredients nourish nature. Nutrients move from the environment into living things to help them thrive. Then, nutrients are recycled back into the planet's land, air, and water. This cycle occurs within Earth's **ecosystems**. Matter and energy flow through these systems as living things feed, digest, and move around. The nutrient cycle has powered our world for a long time. If we protect it, it can help us survive long into the future.

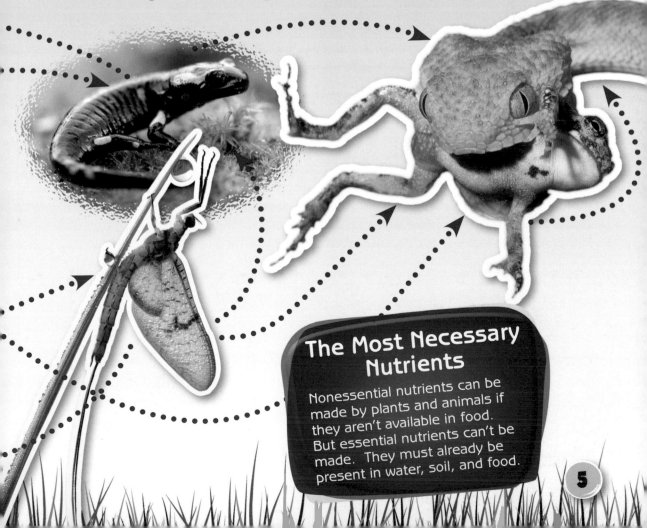

The Most Necessary Nutrients

Nonessential nutrients can be made by plants and animals if they aren't available in food. But essential nutrients can't be made. They must already be present in water, soil, and food.

Water Cycle

The nutrient cycle is made up of smaller cycles. The water cycle is a vital part of this process. Plants and animals (including humans) need water to live. It's essential to our survival. Our bodies are made mostly of water. We need it to keep blood pumping through our bodies. And we need it to create energy. But we're constantly losing water, too. It's important that living things replenish their bodies by drinking water.

Water moves and changes forms in ways that allow us all to survive and thrive. Water can be liquid, like the water in your glass or in the ocean. When water gets hot enough, it turns into a gas, like steam. And when water gets really cold, it can turn into a solid in the form of ice. Other changes might be seen after a storm. You might step in a puddle or see drops forming on leaves. Heat from the sun turns that puddle from a liquid to a gas. This process is called *evaporation*. When these drops rise and cool, they form clouds. The gas turns back into a liquid. This process is called *condensation*.

evaporation

Dino Water

The water you drink today has been around a long time. In fact, it may be the same water that was lapped up by a dinosaur millions of years ago! Of course, this water has been recycled and cleaned naturally.

condensation

Doctors recommend people drink eight glasses of water daily to stay hydrated.

When clouds get too heavy to stay in the air, the droplets fall to the ground. They can fall in the form of rain, sleet, snow, or hail. This is called *precipitation*.

Some rainwater fills up lakes. Some flows into streams and rivers. Then, it gets carried out to the ocean. The sun causes some of the rainwater in those bodies of water to evaporate. And the cycle starts all over again.

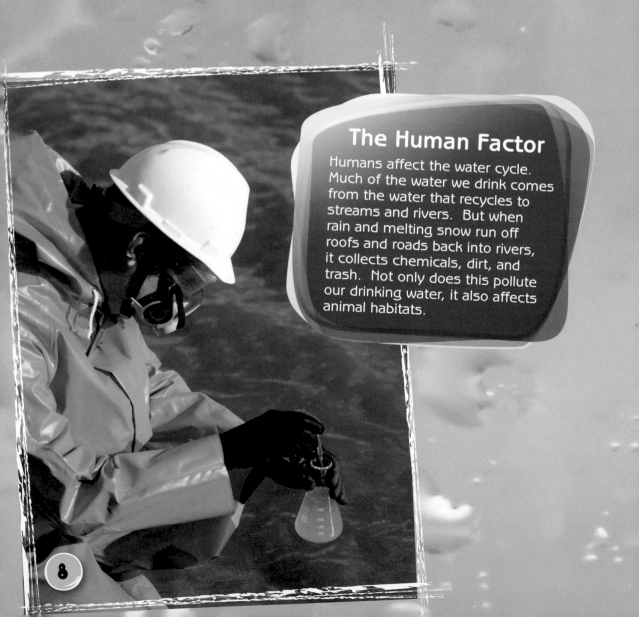

The Human Factor

Humans affect the water cycle. Much of the water we drink comes from the water that recycles to streams and rivers. But when rain and melting snow run off roofs and roads back into rivers, it collects chemicals, dirt, and trash. Not only does this pollute our drinking water, it also affects animal habitats.

Do Plants Sweat?

You probably get a little sweaty when you run. Another word for *sweat* is *perspiration*. Plants do something similar. It's called *transpiration*. It's the process by which plants lose water out of their leaves. This releases water vapor back into the air.

The Clean Water Act was created in 1948 to protect our water supply. Drink up!

Rain and melting snow also soak into the ground. This water seeps into the soil, making water for trees and grass. Soil and sand absorb the water and hold onto it like a sponge. Water moves underground and in between spaces in rocks and soil. This groundwater makes up more than 90 percent of all available freshwater in the world. Groundwater is used by trees, plants, and animals. It can also be stored in an **aquifer**. Many people get the water for their homes from an aquifer. The water cycle recycles water and gives living things the water they need to survive.

Nitrogen Cycle

Water isn't the only thing that nature recycles. Other nutrients also change form and move back and forth between living things and nonliving things. One of them is nitrogen. Nitrogen is all around us. But you'd never know it! This gas has no color, taste, or odor. But 78 percent of the atmosphere is made of it. Nitrogen is one of the most important **elements** on Earth. It's used by all living things. Plants can't grow without it.

Too Much of a Good Thing

The health of the nutrient cycle depends on each type of nutrient being in balance with the others. Too much of one nutrient can produce nutrient pollution.

Nitrogen causes algae to grow much larger than they're supposed to.

Then, algae use all of the oxygen in the water and produce harmful chemicals.

Farmers use fertilizers to add nitrogen to the soil. This helps plants grow larger and faster.

There may be a lot of nitrogen in the air, but most life forms can only use nitrogen in a special form. There are **bacteria** that specialize in producing nitrogen that living things can use. The process starts in the soil. Here, the special bacteria turn the nitrogen into ammonia. (Yes, just like the smelly household cleaner!) But ammonia is better known for killing plants than helping them grow. So another type of bacteria steps in. They turn the ammonia into **nitrates**. And plants can use nitrates! They use nitrates to create **protein**. And protein helps them grow big and strong. Many animals eat plants and get the protein as well. Proteins are then moved to larger animals that eat the protein-rich smaller animals.

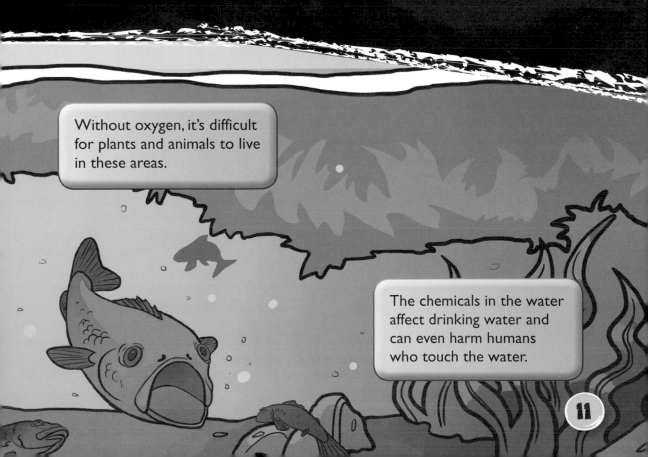

Without oxygen, it's difficult for plants and animals to live in these areas.

The chemicals in the water affect drinking water and can even harm humans who touch the water.

Nitrogen is also a part of chlorophyll. Chlorophyll is found inside plant cells. It is what makes leaves green. It collects energy from the sun and uses it to combine water and **carbon dioxide** to make sugar and oxygen. If there isn't enough nitrogen in chlorophyll, plants suffer. They may stop growing, and their leaves may turn yellow.

But there's more to the nitrogen cycle. When an animal dies, bacteria, worms, and **fungi** go to work. These decomposers help break down dead animals. This allows the nutrients in their bodies to go back into the earth.

Worms munching on a dead animal in the road may look gross. But they're a key part of the nitrogen cycle. The nutrients that go back into the soil can become food for plants and then animals. These decomposers even release nitrogen back into the air. And the cycle starts all over again.

Energy from the Clouds

Lightning storms create a lot of energy. The energy helps oxygen molecules bond to nitrogen molecules to create nitrates that plants can use.

Building Blocks

Atoms bond to form molecules. Elements are different kinds of atoms.

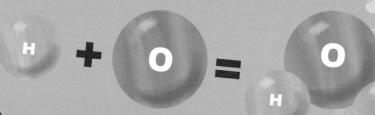

2 hydrogen atoms + 1 oxygen atom = 1 water molecule

An atom is the smallest particle that can exist by itself.

8 protons
8 neutrons

substance

element

molecule

atom

8 electrons

oxygen atom

A molecule is two or more atoms bonded, or stuck, together.

An element is made up of only one kind of atom. Oxygen, carbon, and nitrogen are elements.

Carbon Cycle

Carbon is found in every living thing on Earth. It's part of the air we breathe. It's in the water we drink. It's also in shiny diamonds. It's in the gas in your car. It's even in the pencil you write with! Carbon is one of the most important elements on Earth.

But how do living things get carbon? It starts with **photosynthesis**. First, a plant's roots absorb water and nutrients from soil. Then, plants absorb carbon dioxide (CO_2) through their leaves. Plants use CO_2 and sunlight to make glucose, or sugar. Glucose gives plants fuel to grow.

Carbon gets passed to animals when they eat plants. Animals use carbon to build and repair cells in their bodies. When animals eat other animals, the carbon keeps getting passed along.

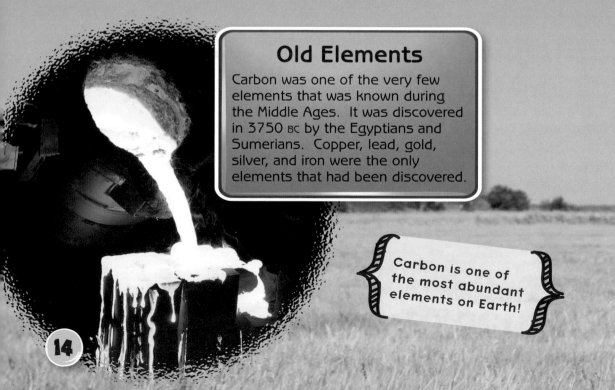

Old Elements

Carbon was one of the very few elements that was known during the Middle Ages. It was discovered in 3750 BC by the Egyptians and Sumerians. Copper, lead, gold, silver, and iron were the only elements that had been discovered.

Carbon is one of the most abundant elements on Earth!

CO₂

Cows get carbon from the plants they eat. They release carbon into the air when they breathe out.

CO₂

The carbon cycle doesn't just involve the movement of carbon as plants and animals are eaten. When you exhale, you return carbon dioxide into the air. But there's also another way that carbon is returned to Earth. When plants and the animals that eat them die and are buried in the ground, they also release carbon. Decomposers break them down and return carbon to the soil. Then, the carbon can be used by more living things. A carbon atom can be used again and again. It recycles itself. It can be part of many different organisms over millions of years!

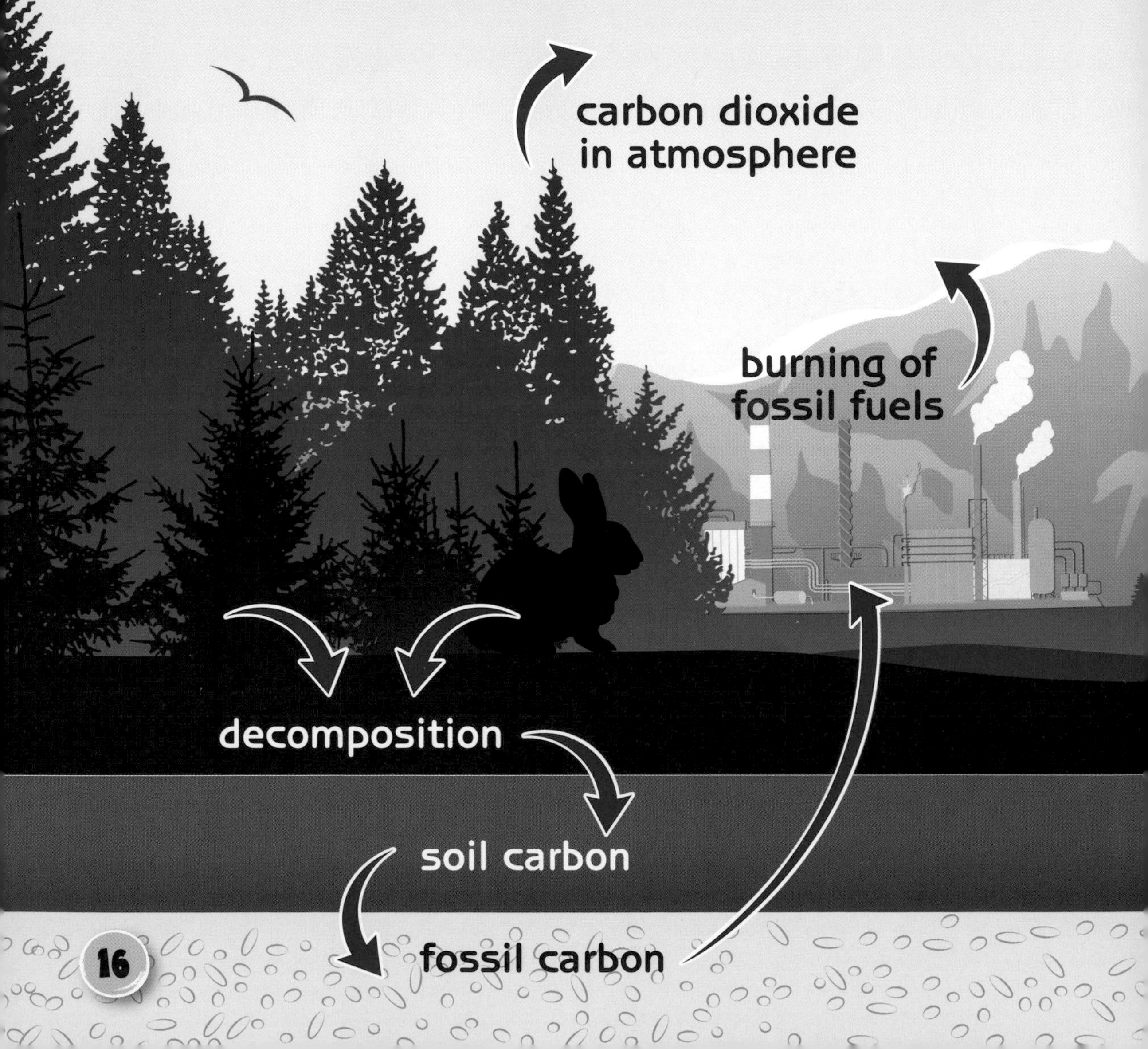

carbon dioxide
in atmosphere

burning of
fossil fuels

decomposition

soil carbon

fossil carbon

But there's a catch. If dead plants and animals are buried too deep, the carbon may get trapped. It might not be able to get to living things. Dead plants and animals trapped deep underground sometimes turn into **fossil fuels**. Coal and oil are two forms of fossil fuels. Carbon dioxide is released into the air when humans burn fossil fuels. Too much carbon dioxide in the atmosphere can change Earth's climate. And the results are serious.

Walking Lighter

When scientists talk about global warming, they often tell people to lower their "carbon footprint." A carbon footprint is the amount of greenhouse gases, such as carbon dioxide, that a person, organization, or country releases into the air.

exhale
carbon dioxide

plant and animal
intake

Fossil fuels take millions of years to form. We use fossil fuels more quickly than they can be created, so now we are running out!

Oxygen Cycle

Take a deep breath in. Now breathe out. Doesn't that feel good? Just about all living things need oxygen to survive. That includes you and me!

Fortunately, there's a lot of oxygen in the air. In fact, 21 percent of the atmosphere is made of this gas. From there, it moves from one living thing to the next. It weaves through the environment and back again. Just like the other cycles we've learned about.

Most oxygen is released into the air by plants. This is part of photosynthesis. Plants turn sunlight into energy by changing carbon dioxide and water into glucose and oxygen. In a way, we can say plants "breathe" in carbon dioxide and "breathe" out oxygen.

Once plants release oxygen, animals and humans breathe it in. Oxygen is then used in our bodies to help break down glucose for fuel. Finally, we breathe out carbon dioxide (just as in the carbon cycle). Carbon dioxide is used over again and again by plants as they release oxygen. The oxygen and carbon cycles weave together to power our world.

Pure Oxygen

Space suits don't just provide oxygen for astronauts to breathe. They also surround astronauts' bodies with oxygen to help maintain regular blood pressure. Instead of air like we have on Earth, astronauts use pure oxygen.

Luckily for You...

There is more oxygen in the atmosphere than almost any other gas. Nitrogen is the only gas there is more of!

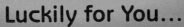

78% NITROGEN

21% OXYGEN

1% OTHER

oxygen

carbon dioxide

Oxygen makes up about 65 percent of the human body. Most of this is found in the form of water.

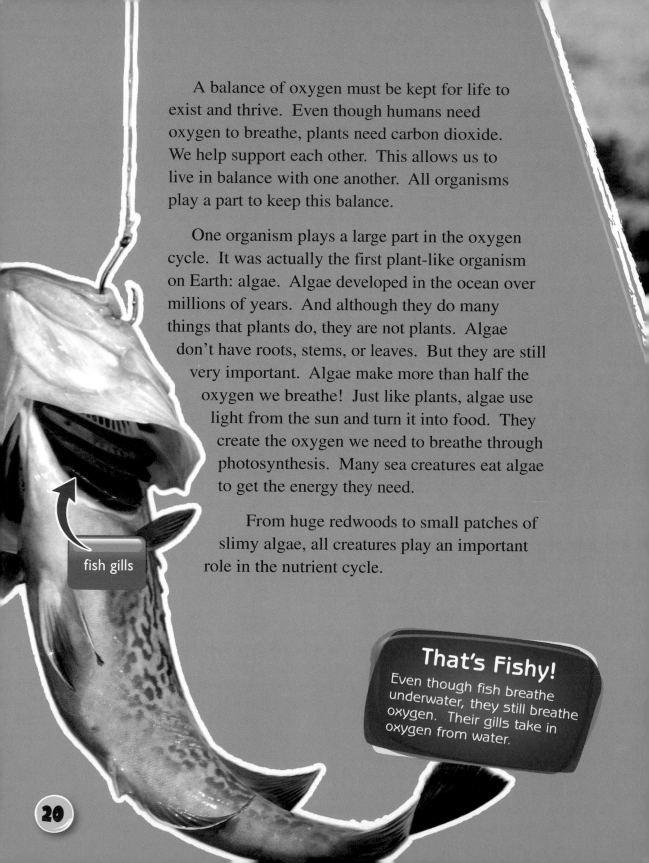

A balance of oxygen must be kept for life to exist and thrive. Even though humans need oxygen to breathe, plants need carbon dioxide. We help support each other. This allows us to live in balance with one another. All organisms play a part to keep this balance.

One organism plays a large part in the oxygen cycle. It was actually the first plant-like organism on Earth: algae. Algae developed in the ocean over millions of years. And although they do many things that plants do, they are not plants. Algae don't have roots, stems, or leaves. But they are still very important. Algae make more than half the oxygen we breathe! Just like plants, algae use light from the sun and turn it into food. They create the oxygen we need to breathe through photosynthesis. Many sea creatures eat algae to get the energy they need.

From huge redwoods to small patches of slimy algae, all creatures play an important role in the nutrient cycle.

fish gills

That's Fishy!
Even though fish breathe underwater, they still breathe oxygen. Their gills take in oxygen from water.

A tiger walks through water with surface algae.

alga under a microscope

Phosphorus Cycle

If someone strikes a match or uses fertilizer in a garden, phosphorus is involved. Phosphorus is an element. It's part of the nitrogen family. However, phosphorus is almost never found in its pure form. It combines with other elements in nature. It's very unstable and flammable. This means it's looking to bond with other elements and can catch fire easily. Not only that, but phosphorus is highly toxic. Phosphorus is important but is one of the scarcest elements.

Some phosphorus compounds are called *phosphates*. Compounds are substances that are created when elements join together. Calcium phosphate is one of the best known. That's the mineral that makes up the bulk of our bones.

Dirty Waters

Phosphorus is like nitrogen. If it gets in the water, it can cause algae to grow too much, decreasing the water's oxygen. You can help prevent nitrogen and phosphorus pollution.

- Use phosphate-free detergents, soaps, and household cleaners.
- Run the washing machine and dishwasher only when full.
- Don't walk your pet near streams or other water bodies.
- Pick up after your pet.
- Turn electronics off or unplug them when you aren't using them.
- Open shades for sunlight instead of turning on lights.

Phosphorus is constantly recycled by Earth and moves through a cycle. Phosphorus is released when a rock erodes due to wind, water, or other natural forces. Plants absorb phosphorus from soil and water. Animals get phosphorus from the plants they eat. Other animals get it from the animals they eat. Animals return phosphorus to the environment in their waste or when they decay after dying.

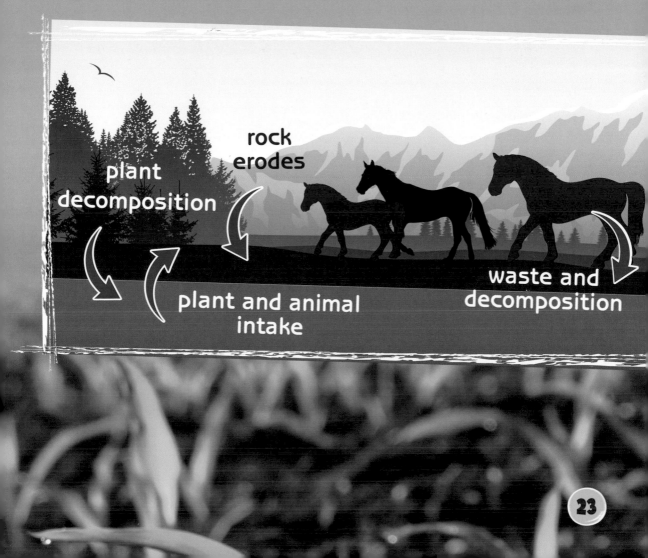

plant decomposition

rock erodes

plant and animal intake

waste and decomposition

Untangling the Food Web

Without water, nitrogen, oxygen, or phosphorus, there could be no life on Earth. And without these cycles, these essential substances would be used up after a single use. But instead, these cycles continue to support one another. All the cycles that make up the nutrient cycle have something in common. They're all connected to food chains. Food chains show the flow of energy through an ecosystem.

In a food chain, plants absorb energy from the sun and turn it into fuel. From tiny insects to huge elephants, all kinds of animals eat plants for nourishment. That's how they get their energy. Some animals get energy by eating other animals. When animals die, decomposers break down whatever nutrients are left and return them to the soil. Those nutrients become food for plants to use. And the cycle begins again.

When food chains grow complex, they are called *food webs*. Often in an ecosystem, each living thing is part of many food chains. The food chains branch out in many directions. They crisscross and overlap. When you look at all the interconnected food chains, you end up with something that looks more like a spiderweb.

Changing the Food Web

Hunting is the cause of many animals' extinctions. When that happens, other animals aren't able to get the nutrients they need, and they die out, too. Now, there are laws to regulate hunting. We also protect animals that are endangered.

A plant gets energy from the sun and the soil.

A grasshopper eats the plant.

A cougar eats the fox.

A mouse eats the grasshopper.

A fox eats the mouse.

A Neverending Cycle

Life on Earth revolves around a few invisible but essential nutrients. The most important nutrients are water, carbon, oxygen, nitrogen, and phosphorus. They each have their own purpose. But they are also interconnected. The cycles of these nutrients need to stay in perfect balance for the planet to thrive. Knowing how these cycles work—and how human behavior affects them—can help us protect nature's balance.

"When we try to pick out anything by itself, we find it hitched to everything else in the universe."
—John Muir, conservationist

Think Like a Scientist

How do chemicals enter groundwater, and what effect do they have on Earth's cycles? Experiment and find out!

What to Get

- clear plastic cup
- food coloring
- food wrappers and other trash
- soil, sand, and pebbles
- vegetable oil
- water

What to Do

1 Pour a layer of sand into the cup. Then, add the soil and the pebbles. Carefully fill the cup halfway with water.

water
pebbles
soil
sand

2 One by one, add food coloring, vegetable oil, and trash into the cup. Observe what happens to the water after each item is added. Record your observations in a chart like the one below.

	Green Food Coloring (pesticides/fertilizer)	Vegetable Oil (motor oil)	Soil, Sand, and Pebbles	Trash
Color				
Thickness				
Natural?				
Removable?				

3 Try to remove the items from the water. In your chart, record what was easy to remove and what was difficult.

4 Discuss the effect each item would have on plant and animal life. Which items are added to water naturally? Which items are added by people?

Glossary

aquifer—layers of rock or sand that can absorb and hold water

bacteria—tiny organisms that break down dead plants and animals

carbon dioxide—a gas that is produced when people and animals breathe out or when certain fuels are burned

ecosystems—everything that exists in particular environments

elements—basic substances that are made of atoms of only one kind and that cannot be separated by ordinary chemical means into simpler substances

fossil fuels—fuels that are formed in Earth from dead plants or animals

fungi—organisms that do not have chlorophyll and eat nonliving matter

nitrates—chemical compounds that contain oxygen and nitrogen and are used in fertilizer

nutrients—substances that living things need to grow

photosynthesis—the process in which plants use sunlight to combine water and carbon dioxide to make their own food (glucose)

protein—substance found in meat, beans, and nuts that helps build up the tissues in living things

Index

Your Turn!

Everyday Evidence

Find evidence of Earth's cycles in your everyday life. Does the water cycle make puddles on the playground? Are the bugs in your garden working hard for the nutrient cycle? Write a list of the evidence you find. How are these cycles related to one another?